Everything Smells Like Rain

JR Hataway

Cover photo: Nur Andi Ravsanjani Gusma

WE MEET AGAIN

I welcome you to this chapter of my writing journey. I believe *Everything Smells Like Rain* showcases the growth I've experienced in the never-ending quest to find my own voice in the world of poetry.

Throughout this book there are pieces consisting of ten lines, five "couplets" if you will. This is a variation on one of the oldest forms of Arabic poetry, the ghazal (pronounced "guzzle"). Poet Jim Harrison adopted a form of this style ignoring rhyme and meter but focusing on tying the couplets together metaphorically. I challenged myself by tackling this form and as a result I see my poetry through a new lens. I truly hope you enjoy it as much as I have.

The pages to follow are lined with my heart and soul so I invite you to take your time and enjoy *Everything Smells Like Rain*.

As Always, For Rae

That girl with sunrise in her eyes

With eyes of daylight
she greets me
wearing dawn like a jewel

CONTENTS

Storms I chase leave
nowhere to run...

Photo by Max Bender

Everything Smells Like Rain

I wake to thunder's musical melancholy
an unseen thrashing somewhere in the world
confining me to corridors contrived of books unread

Bickering hours are eddies in the river
as unchained dogs take human shape
rooting through debris along the shore
waters I tread have messy edges

There are no definitive answers
in the drum of an untamed heart
storms I chase leave nowhere to run
and today, everything smells like rain

Unoriginal Poetry

I crawl out of my den
kid from nowhere ready to binge
on the next series of dreams

I swing on a low sweetgum branch
just to straighten my back
it's stiff and bent from sleeping in a chair

Issuing my cries as soon as the moon is in tune
that carrier of light sits like a star on my shoulder

Life has a way of spreading you out
things make less sense
clarity of resolution just out of reach
mud on a turtle's back

Aimless is my dance

unoriginal poetry convincing no one

black-eyed promises fade like taillights

in the swirling dust of a slow drive

taking the long way home

Photo by Hanna

A Nearness So Far

My track tears a wound across the water
engines hum in rhythm with my yearning
a crumpled cadence in the salt of my wake

I taste the time in the bleak wind
until the darkness is used up
beneath that garden of dry stars
taunting with a nearness so far
and I put your name in another song

Now the sun stains my morning
its handiwork the dust of a kiss
and I hang this dream
from the last slice of the moon

Sudden and Slow

Dark is the joy at 1 am hopping aboard my pen
unbound poetry and worn floorboards under bitter incandescence

Sudden and slow in their return
are failures I'd just as soon forget

Innate delusions dilute my song
swept along as if fired from a slingshot

Wandering worries become rips in my jeans
in the briar patch where the blackberries hang out

It will be alright- soaking up my share of the night
because the moon, she never picks sides

Shut Up and Watch

Crushing air looks for someone to blame
fragile chaos becomes a theory on life

Imposed norms cost a fortune
I have mountains of books to help me disappear

My feet drag along the path
where my hands create a paper trail

Time is wasted with songs about what isn't fair
still I'm muddled in tangents to heal these doubts

So who am I to get mad when the moon
tells me to shut up and watch?

Dollar Bill Wind

Today was warm, a false season
now as evening falls words are working on me
I'm squeezing another dream from this paper
I need its patience and forgiveness

Mixed up in the same dark
I'm wondering which star is the newest pebble in the road
assigning them names drawn from my own existence
heavy steps where snow played soft on the hill where we held on

Last night the wind blew circles tearing like a dollar bill
but tonight the moon is a purring cat
nestled in her bed

Scattered Wishes

Accompany me in a little respite
from the absurdity of the world
laying circles in the meadow
where the white coin moon
reveals our likeness to the gods

Falling stars cut the cold
swinging from the sky
and scattered wishes are sown seeds
where hearts leap in the blossoms and breeze

So I ask who better than me,
the hopeless poet before you,
could grind your fears to dust
and ignite the dreams
that dance in your hair?

FALL FROM THE SKY

I craft another argument with reality
poetry defunct in a raging dream

A slave to whispers only I can hear
whispers these walls will never understand

Tonight brings detachment between heart and head
like waiting for words to fall from the sky

I climb that hill where the moon plays like a jukebox
and fireflies pitch a game of horseshoes

Just to shuffle my feet in a race with dawn
and kick my own dent in the world

Stash of Glory

There's a steady wind rocking the trees
turning the night on its head
storms roll in on my last stash of glory
leaving me as blue as a distant mountain

The search for light is dire
in the dark forest of the soul
I'm steadily striking matches
trying to find my own name

It's in these times I feel cursed
bound to merely scratch the surface of things
a two-wheel drive on a steep gravel road
my only choice is mash the gas and give it hell

KEEP MY SONG PLAIN

So much of the world has rusted in time
cramped logic stiffens my features
synthetic thoughts stain my countenance
even the birds seem to sleepwalk

Reduced to a ghost in a real setting
needing refuge from this technicolor riot
some scrap of frontier to find peace in my hour

I float on southward and keep my song plain
a whiskey-soaked poet with old man river's beard
midnight on my shoulders like a cloak
following constellations of discarded gods

Uncertain Fire

Day rumbles by as if time is horse-drawn
embroiled in fantasy where lost identity
is a crown of praise

Call me out of this dark corner
sentences here hit hard
they'll claw your eyes out
if you let them

Just let me make it to midnight
when the moon drifts through
measuring the width of the cold
and I'm measuring my footsteps
like a car across frosted ground

Deep as a Bone

A hard rain falls through the clouds
setting the stage for my spare time to fly

I keep digging for something just out of reach
deep as a bone next to nothing

Meager is this counterfeit, like pawn shop jewelry
a plan to understand is another fool's errand

Tinge my days with gold, for the wind is listening
and these ghosts wield knives that sing

I'll pour out what was so carefully bottled up
a dark base for reflections to rage

Cold Flame

Spring has the river ready to brawl
chained down by money I'm ready to rage

I plant a garden of images in ten pounds of dust
draping them in moonbows, that jewelry of dreams

A cold flame of sadness lies on my tongue
but even a snake knows not to poison itself

There's a cryptic refrain behind my mirror
and I need to clean the rust off my hammer

Ungag my soul so I can tear this silence apart
like the wind in its costume of thunder

Drunken Linguist

My thoughts rust like iron in vinegar
attached to outcomes dependent on a cycle of good and bad

At the hilltop of a dream I scoop out a grave
where the moon's rays play as softly as the sleep of a flower

Mincing my words like a drunken linguist mad in the sun
now night places her coins over my eyes

Misery has a hair trigger in time's garden
and I'm pounding rocks from my plow

Waves don't have to be water to erode stone
that's my handwriting right there on the wall

Running With Eyes Closed

Pulling his nose from a book

A boy opens the window

to let the pages breathe

alone in a room quiet as the stars

he is sick with the disease of a dreamer

Unsure of right or real

artificial flowers and photo album heartbreak

running with eyes closed

through the shotguns and guitars

Grandfather is hard of hearing

and mother is getting married again

spirit diminishing like smoke

grabbing at the wind

You learn to protect what water you have

when the house is always on fire

Photo by Marek Piwnicki

Slow Machine

I come and go from the world
keeping my stories behind a fear to speak
a tumultuous dance under wrinkled sky,
that bedsheet that won't flatten,
where dust falls through when the day
goes into the ground

If luck is with me, I'll borrow a shade of mercy
from this night and pluck love right from the vine
hide me from the voices of the earth
and their bonfire of sound; It hurts my head

Answers bled from the slow machine
are both glorious and terrifying
I've the latest fancy gadget to turn them into poems
but you'll need to strike a match to read them

Shattered Sameness

It's three in the morning and I've pen in hand
struck by an urgency to get this down
if only I knew what it was

Harsh lighting mimics the mood,
a perspective undoctored,
to craft beauty from pain in all of night's colors

Soon the unburied dead
will fire up their metal coffins
clogging the road between where I've been
and where I want to go

But for now the stars are singing their old ballad
and I'm swerving in the shattered sameness
that brushes against my wheels

Unborn Flowers

Snoring dog at my feet; purring cat at my shoulder
all of us waiting for the sun to dry out the world

A battle rages with blank lines on paper
life's obligations clog my head; this could get bloody

Want and illusion kick the can down the road
windfall fruits of a wistful mind

Words are grating stones rubbing together
we'll see if the noise and dust pull a poem out of me

I've books by my chair and coffee on its flat arm
I can afford to be silent while unborn flowers
seek out the right dirt

Check Engine Light

Narrative arcs along the last phase of eclipse
bones in the rain swallowed by an ocean of promise

Behind the thin disguise of make believe
imagined freedoms are just meat to distract the dog

Outnumbered, like a bullied child on the playground
just wanting out, plugging keys into every fake door

Cluttered shelves strain from the weight
pulling nails from dreams about the next shiny thing

I cover my check engine light with black tape
and voice my grievances right into the steering wheel

Words That Scratch

Idleness lights a fire in my belly
must I always poetize words that scratch?
mixing different shades in search of true colors
images I prod until they roar like lions

Maybe I'll build a myth with the daisies at dawn
those black-eyed sisters well aware
ghosts don't rest easy

Tip-toeing wears holes into my socks
the past is so easily stirred up
just as an old song knocks memories loose
to fall like pebbles at your feet

I laugh when the poets say "just be true"
or "write from the heart "
my paper is crumbling from the weight of so much truth
and I must not forget to make it weird
for my imaginary friends
they wouldn't have it any other way

Cold Light of the Battlefield

Couplets and quatrains lie strewn about
across my last acre of moonlight
I'm biting my knuckles for them
to take on a life of their own

I sit by the river
that black artery draining its water
thrumming in resonance with stars
that sing in my blood

Taps of silence count off like heartbeats
as animals in the dark grow restless
their nightly whispers hungry
for the cold light of the battlefield

Mercy is a dark cousin whose face I've yet to meet

a steady diet of flowers and knives

will keep my identity quiet

trusting only gravity to hold me down

Photo by Vincent M.A. Janssen

Haiku

Lover to the stars
seeks poetry in shadows
sculpted in moonlight...

Equal damage is done
be it sharpened pencil or loaded rifle
I can shoot the heart right out of the night
either way is nothing new to me
regret is fleeting like money
spent on easily broken things
I used to have a machine that played night sounds
to help me sleep but broke
now I just sleep outside
closure is a myth but you get over things
when the ghosts get busy somewhere else
words and dogs haunt my corner of the world

strays looking for a place to call home
just let me catch my breath between dreams
crickets in their odd grace sing their latest tune
their time signature keeps me hanging on edge
like ashes on a forgotten cigarette, ready to fall
the rain has stopped for the first time in days
and I can feel a midnight walk coming on
the road holds water so I can clean my shoes
down where the poles that prop up the power line
lean over with age around the bend
like a smile with crooked teeth
this ramble is long
and I get it if you didn't make it this far
I guess I'll never get the hang of haikus

My Own Harvest

Hope tells a flattering tale
as I nail myself to the wall

Let the words fall out of my head
splattering the page to be sparsely read

Truth parades as fiction
unless it's the other way around

Unraveling in order across fate's tinted glass
shapes justified in their own reflection

My own harvest I'll soon reap
a collection of roses I intend to burn

Blind Collaboration

Morning greets me in her stillness
nothing shaking but the leaves on the trees

Struck cold by the sight of dark clouds west of here
thundering a song so often misunderstood

I've no love for sterile days
pour yellow on this blue and I'll take all the green

Childhood memories kick like a mule
and I can already taste the rain on my lips

Set my heart to dance in blind collaboration
across an empty canvas I could never bog down with a name

The Clock Ties Everything Down

The clock ties everything down
desperate is this song of time travel

To get lost in the trees
where fireflies play hide and seek
and poems hit the ground like pears
but only when they're ready

So I wait- nestled in the fury
of a world with no patience
bound to rip some beauty
from an imperfect narrative

Swimming against a current
of missed appointments and expiring passwords

longing for the sweet taste of the shore
where worries dry in the sun

I dance along charred edges of the latest golden age
covering my tracks like a wanted man
nothing more to do when the clock
ties everything down

Photo by Sare Akin

Painfully Misunderstood

Dark is the joy at 1 am hopping aboard my pen
Unbound poetry and worn floorboards under bitter incandescence

Sudden and slow in their return
are failures I'd just as soon forget

Innate delusions dilute my song
swept along as if fired from a slingshot

Wandering worries become rips in my jeans
in the briar patch where the blackberries hang out

It will be alright- soaking up my share of the night
because the moon, she never picks sides

Soak in the Mystery

Signal fades in the heaviest air
as the whippoorwill grows tired of its song

I had no intention to drink until morning
the sharp scent of bewilderment spins me counterclockwise

Left to soak in the mystery of muddy names
wiping their feet on other names

The heat of dreams leathers my skin
and ties my bootlaces together

I fill the pages of journals just to find I'm a stranger to myself
so I call it poetry

Garbage Day

I procrastinate until the day gets hot
then bitch about the heat
my story is written
trying to rationalize things to myself

I made chicory coffee by accident
I wanted regular- now I can see around corners

It's garbage day so I check the mail
some cult is having a membership drive
the fire in my head doesn't need more fuel,
just a break in the wind to let these ashes
fertilize the ground

I'm beyond weary of choosing sides
both belonging to the same fake coin

We're landlocked here
so there's no tide to blame
just hope that stars on the other side of the abyss
can keep it all sewn together

Steal me a few hours from this absurdity
I'll dig out the closet where moths chew holes in my hat
I dream of running time backwards
not to escape the pains of age,
or to choose the winning numbers,
but to unlearn what is useless to know

Moments of harmony within a cacophony of noise
cling to me like ivy up a stone wall
And it's within these truths
I'll duel to the death
like expensive boots that still hurt your feet
and sad eyes that cannot tell a lie

Strange Gods

Winter is finally gone and I wonder
which way my song will turn
How many layers can I peel away
for shadows no longer cold?

I walked the road this morning
my lost necklace nowhere to be found
all I saw was a hubcap tucked away like money
hidden so well you never find it again

The tractor is finally paid off
but now it needs to go to the shop
and the humidity keeps my cheap guitar
horribly out of tune- both signs of the times I guess

There are some tough rows to hoe
on a farm of fixed ideas- always plowing
for some spark of reason
poetry in perfect disorder

Dreams are strange gods
and masters of their own meaning
I sit back and let fate blow the dust off
the book of rules meant to be broken

Cold Feet

Lightning through the window
lights up my book of pretty words
trying to get something, anything, down
in a self-imposed race with dawn

Staining my teeth in coffee's fluid comfort
waiting out this storm to see if poetry
can raise its voice over the din

My thunder-frightened dog
whimpers under the table
but the cat, with eyes half-open, is unmoved
like a church ignoring a beggar

Soon the sun will break through,
birds will knock wet branches out of the way,
and I'll cover my cold feet
in socks that don't match

Another page will be added
to a gallery of frameless art
lost time I tend to justify
by the flimsiest of reasons

Sunday Morning

Another car flies down my road
gravel pings steel in a mad dash for church
late for the saving

Light beer promises of Saturday night
track footprints on Sunday morning
mice in a maze viewing the sky in pieces

Distractions jam up my mind
like vacationers at a toll booth
thoughts are tangled vines
my notebook a weigh station of dreams

The yard around my house is a live with birds
a talking garden where I throw poetry like seed
all of us having something to say

and no control over what ears will do the hearing

and I for one am good with that

Photo by Dave Hoefler

Raw Materials

I woke up wondering what color is your sky?
I know it could never match the promise of your eyes
as it unfurls over that cathedral of clouds

Merging traffic keeps my foot pinned to the floor
each thought becoming a grave
as miles click away under my heels

The curse of the poet knows not where to begin
but cherry-picks truths from each sleepless night
and pulls every apology from the rain

Raw are these materials laced upon the savage fire I now feed
light to see me safely home
where time always stands still
in the wake of your smile

WORTHLESS WISDOM

My last cool breath is traded with the night
she departs, leaving me with a half-moon smile

Here comes the sun to scratch my hide
breaking rainbows like wishbones
drying out the mud where I intend to plant roses
an insignia of woundless scars braided in the wind

Poetry becomes a basket for every egg I can find
a wealth of worthless wisdom funneled into generic art

Some pray for rain while others dig a well
and I'm bound to dance between the two
But I can close my eyes see stars anytime I want
so maybe that counts for something

El Gato Negro

I keep my seat and stay my breath, for now
soon that black cat will cross my road

Night is sliced by straight-line stars
turns out they're satellites; more junk for an already loaded sky

The moon is my friend but a little jealous at times
looting the page where I lay my tongue down

With each tick of the heart
the baggage of words grows more attuned to the current

Though my bones they creak with the walls that try to hold me
like a candle in the rain I will always dance to the sound of water

Photo by Marek Piwnicki

Soul Song

This poet is blind

Give me something to shield my eyes
as I break the north point of morning

Another checkpoint on a road of days
between dawn's violet epiphany
and that ancient god setting the world on fire

Birds call me to order
a soul song bright and lonesome
waltzing along the shoulder of the hill
a perfect mix of holy and crazy

I pull on the clean air until it hurts
and life's vicious circle eases its grip on my neck
never could I hold poetry to form
when shadows are cast like dice from cold hands
and whispered reflections are at least a mile wide

WHEN COWS FLY

Spring revives last year's flowers
and crickets rub their thighs in the pines
excuse me while I fall back into the familiar

Rattling the same chains,
selfish hands exaggerate the obvious
repeating myself ad nauseam
but I'm too confused as to where the new beauty is

The prettiest butterfly I've ever seen
was eating his fill on a dead animal
I still think about it

I turn off the news and find some music
work boots shuffle to Armageddon's tune
I sing of revolution but only amongst friends

Imaginary solutions to shake the sun loose

Another green light is spent for a turn against red
lies masquerade as the key to the dream
just getting by becomes an art in and of itself

Photo by Stijn Dijkstra

A wise man taught me never get mad
if a bird shits on you
because we're lucky cows don't have wings
so I guess it doesn't take much to make me happy

JANITOR

Sharks are swirling the water
like poems that lost their meaning

The sand is so hot it smokes
burning my toes like the ashes of roses

Time goes soft and the wind is a wheezing breath
laughing in your face

But when the sun finally abandons the day
the sky becomes a cold stew of diamonds

It's my time to sweep up the pieces strewn
a janitor of adverbs on a highway to nowhere

Wild and High

A tempest in my teapot blows the morning wide open
lately I count days like spots on the wall
filling my ears with white noise to smooth out my head
the name tied to me has no handle to grasp

A bird just flew into my shed and is beating at the window
desperate like a man out of work, a dollar closer to broke

Wild and high is the grass at my door
worn path winds like a mountain road
where my cat stalks in wait between the fence and forever

With a gentle wave of the broom my good deed is done
and my friend sings with new meaning
from the safety of the trees
He'll no doubt change his tune when he realizes cats can climb

READY FOR WAR

Pull a random book from a random shelf
to a random page I turn
randomness for my random head

It's Sunday-last day to get the yard work done
feels like being sent to cut my own switch
I'd rather sit and come up with fancy words
to cuss the heat

Milking the morning's last breeze
from the only shade I can find
the sun's already cooking the smell out of the dirt
the man in the moon cut out long ago
before his shoes melted

My back is turned on the plans I made
the way youth turned its back on me
but maybe this drought will starve planted fears
rooted so deep

There must be something to quell this thirst
because the tv just tells me get ready for war
armchair revolutionaries wouldn't know love
if it hit them square in the face

But it's love, and only love, for which I fight
drawn out through the sweat and tears
imposing my tongue in poetry of bloody knuckles

Tired of Flowers

The chicken snake scales the wall
cool to the touch where shadows are empty

Sleeplessness makes my eyes burn
as an unconscious hymn burns the back of my throat

I'm thankful that silence is moon-shaped
every time the cannon scares the deer out of the corn

Shattering dreams that fragment into echoes
like a butterfly finally tired of flowers

I can always zoom in to avoid the big picture
extracting new meaning from context I can't explain

Photo by Nandhu Kumar

WASTED MUSINGS

Word pictures dwell in the smallest of spaces
a good enough vocation for the bad son I guess

The theory of light is no match for winds of old age
I've a mountain of wasted musings
from digging a hole to hell with a feather

The summer night draws blood
as I lean out the driver's side
nicknaming each air pocket every twenty feet
desperate for a punchline
but like a cheap stamp licked one too many times
they don't stick around for long

Useless Statistics

Dreams are merely a point of departure
in the art of saying one thing and meaning another

Symbols of a cruel revolution
all decked out in bad grammar

I hit my head on memories stacked like stones in a low archway
the blood of yesterday's scars matts my hair

Useless statistics rob me of a clear view
leaving me narrow-sighted in a forest of images

Ignoring the body's advice I pull soul from the moon
as long as tears continue to taste just like the sea

Letter to Sunset

Sunset yesterday was beautiful
if only you could have seen it
pastel colors slung all over the sky
as silos and a barn on some Illinois farm
stood in proud silhouette

One of those sunsets that keeps poets up at night
or pulls a new song out of some whiskey-soaked troubadour

But me? I kept driving
my obligation to keep the lights on held my foot on the gas
as the scenery tied my heart in knots
from my rear-view mirror
clouded by the dust of discontent
across my back window

It's been said that life punishes the vague wish
and rewards the specific ask
just remember they killed Socrates
for asking too many questions

My dreams have never lacked definition
they branch out of me, growing every direction
and like knots in a pine log burn brightest
every time I set them on fire

So I share with you my letter to sunset
and of the magic still holding my breath hostage

Poetry, for me at least, can be an exercise
of juggled exaggerations
and I'll plead guilty as charged
also guilty of letting the madness
of the world's deadlines box me in
on the fast lane at 80 mph

Sunset yesterday was truly something to see
and I've nothing to share but the memory
so this blank page will have to suffer the consequences

Dreams of Remedies

I woke this morning to see the poets fighting again
two poems by the same title, alike but different
some try to corner the market on ideas
while others just need to be better thieves
my heroes mastered both

An ill wind blows dust off the gods
they hang like old traffic lights in a city of chains
confusion flops like a bird inside me
all up in this misery
where dreams of remedies crowd out the days

Snakes are drunk from pollution in the river
I walk a mile back and forth along the bank
wiping sweat and digging lashes out of eyes
I need to see

I should be working or writing a letter to my boss
July has arrived but my raise has not
what's good for him should be good for me

I keep looking over my shoulder
at just who I'm supposed to be
spent pages that once burned as a beacon in fog
are now scattered embers swirling like a cigarette
dropped on the highway

I mustn't shy away from these verses I give you
unavoidable, like bad weather, they're always there
and like the books I carry get heavy as hell

Perhaps I should just keep them private
like my conversations with the moon
or the green-eyed melodies that always sing me to sleep
but then again, who am I kidding

Holes in my Boots

Low is the moon teasing the ground
a warm hug to this wine-soaked delirium

Variety while spicing things up
is crucial to the chaos
I swap out dilemmas like flea market paperbacks

Time is a priceless commodity
that nickels and dimes us to death
my credit maxed out
on this last stretch of freedom

A young groom once promised the world
now needs that world to slow down
for him to read over its shoulder

I'm here taping up the holes in my boots
I have some daisies to plant
we'll dance all night while the beans soak
and wait for the next hero to let us down

Punch Drunk

I watch a hawk glide, snake in his grasp
there's no question what his days are for

His cries of gratitude drown in diesel hum
my red monstrosity crawls like fire across the pasture
I'm brewing on a past that's already passed
and other jokes I know by heart

Stretching stories across the acres
corner-to-corner
a process guaranteed to leave me punch drunk

Tripping forward on the way back
luck is pulled tighter than guitar strings
I just keep avoiding number 13
and trying not to sweeten my tea with salt

Motorized Fate

A new nightmare bares its teeth
I dream of my vessel going down
lifeline frayed in the wind

Are we okay or is it just what we say?
Everyone talks so much it loses meaning
no opinion can force a flower to bloom

Droning voices box me in, stacked and laced
like the cinder blocks of my childhood home
every wall painted with nonsense

The hard seed of the past splits wide open
buried in the pages of my motorized fate
but there's comfort in knowing words
will never command the moonlight

Subtle as Thunder

Through a thousand dreams I pieced us together
standing upon my words and staring down never

The pleasures of the body and their usual taste
hold no candle to sips of the sun's gold
and the sea's emerald sway
hope was tied around the stars and bent over for the moon
that first kiss was as subtle as thunder

Now you're dancing through the rooms
and I'm cleaning tomato soup off the wall
you'd been here a thousand times
before I saw your face or knew your name

You dance through every room
and I'll never be on time for work again

No Purer Sound

Winter rain, so loud on my tin roof
its verse repeating cold and angry

A dancing double-dare to venture outside
with the pressure of a wasted day

Foggy windows mirror my thoughts
as restlessness swallows all that I am

Let this song fall for there's no purer sound
tell me a story and let me sleep

Because, like the stones around my flowerbed,
there's just nothing for me to do right now

Closet Poetry

There is no plan to understand,
only to split the airwaves
when the juice of fermented fruit
does its thing

The fireflies stay put
yellow stars in the field
and the trees are sleeping witnesses
they're all used to this by now

Never accused of lacking intensity
I take off down the road
with no headlights, ticking off miles
like breaths between screams

I have my own ways to cope

when it gets too loud

dressing the walls in closet poetry

but not to worry

I'll beg no one to remember my name

Photo by Tony Phan

UNDERDRESSED

I had a dream I was a king
lost inside a rose
looking for the sun

Relearning the song
of the scatterbrained fool
all chords dissonant like a hungry cat

I woke to luxury of cool linen pinning me down
and it'll take all the horses
to pull me from this bed

I must brave the sneers
a kid on his first day in a new school
underdressed with no invitation to the soirée
but it's fine...

my muse wears the moon like my old shirt
and the best poems hiding in the tall grass
tickle her bare feet

Crack My Tongue Open

A dead pine lies like a fallen column
the gladiators of this capitol city
get scarce when I step so heavily

The pressure to join the fray
steals my breath
I live on silence at least for today

The poet doesn't pray,
the dancer is full of hesitation,
and the audience has no remorse
unless it's trending
no one flattens pennies on railroad tracks anymore

I'll be here until I can taste the morning
and gargle the lies that tumble out of tomorrow
maybe that will crack my tongue open
and I'll tell my story backwards

The Moon Never Sleeps

A murmuration of starlings dances for sunset
winding choreography, like seeds thrown at the sky

I leap to join but fall back against the earth
reality has a way of soiling the skin of things

Lock me in a room full of fancy dreams
my miles of ink will fit through the keyhole

Passions are destitute in the garden of my mind
but for her the moon never sleeps, thankfully

She commands the fireflies with an evening promise
and the morning dandelions to let it all go with a shrug

The Season's Latest Grays

The month of January has left its chill behind
clipping me in a cold silence I wear like cuff-links
and dressing this solitude in the season's latest grays

I stoke the fires to melt the words out of my head
as shadows of my heart become wrinkled sounds
passing room to room

I've no choice but to dream
as I sort through what to keep
and what to let go
clothing this love in a language
that will consume my forevers

Small Deceit

I'm under no pressure to deliver
but I hold myself under the gun
my own small deceit
to write this right

Hovering in discontent of separation
seeking natural rhythms
behind each cut of clouds
holding my breath for each starry reunion

Indifferent to the air that stiffens my bones
I give myself over to mad poetics
wrested from self doubt
borrowing words from the thunder and pain
that dance on my chest

THIN AIR

Look at all those trees

baring it all; pawing at the sky

frostbitten sentries...

calling the centuries home

trading high-fives with the winter wind

I've nothing but respect

for these warriors of time

but, with my collar up to the cold

I'll keep my hands buried in pockets

knowing how it feels

to grasp at thin air

White Lily Moon

Echoes fill this hollow chamber
these questions I pry wide open
existence is a feast of empty calories
and scraps are kicked under the table

Bread scornfully broken under a White Lily moon

Growing wise to the lies I fall to my senses
and things I'm afraid to say pour like liquid gold
or black coffee
I've built a bridge out of love letters
right over the stars to where dreams end

It's In this solitude more my own
I dance in the place I got old
where it stays green year-round

Nothing Else

Wait for me
through the decline and renewal
fashioning so purely
each invented memory

Find me in the endless nuance
and commotion of the rain
waist-deep in all the things
they told us were true

Sing to me and fill this hollow room
of futile pleasures squeezed
from the marrow of the unspoken

Then laugh with me
because there's nothing else we can do

Run Up to the Sky

I long for something to tear away this gray
it slows the hour and colors my mind,
a mind fashioning thoughts
out of memories and traces of places
all made of shipwrecks

I've grown pale as a ghost
as only derelict lines flow
from a broken keyboard
and only shadows fall
when I shake my pen

So stir me up in the sun
like the wind that dances along the river
we can both run up to the sky

Meandering Song

Night hangs about me
a meandering song draping like a robe
as verses blindly multiplied
are wind on the page

Withdrawing hours
tinge my window with dawn
and yesterday's murmurs
would love nothing more
than to fill another day

There's a comedy somewhere
in this meaningless grind
of dreams that keep me awake
weighing me down like a stone
when I want nothing more than to float

FIERY GHOST

Themes recur, nothing I can do about it
maybe you've noticed
maybe not

My heroes taught me poetry is action
but this one dance is all I know

A fool under the sun
writing to my celestial kin
scorning the trifle when the juice
isn't worth the squeeze

Concentrated images cloud up like mirrors
for love songs written in breath on glass

I pass time in these dark halls
the moon teasing the window
that fiery ghost
with eyes to swallow me whole

Last night I woke from a dream
and tattooed it right on my arm
and tonight every light in the house is on

Softly Held Stories

Truths drug out of me
get stacked in the corners of the night
where softly held stories
are an anvil on my head

I've no time for reason
and its dead ends
peace is too important
and dreams have long fingers

We swim through the air
at the weeping heart of things
ghosts in a spectral dance
picking the locks to portals of the unseen

We'll fly like time

and block yesterday's number

bathing in the uncreated light of love's uproar

our eyes sewn shut to the dawn

Un-Strict Stoic

I must pry up the boards to my strip of floor
and step out of my heart
a heart haunted by the face of my father,
a face haunted by all those wasted years,
a haunting that slumbers in my soul

I meet up with a revolving sky
down at the corner of midnight
where the stars are always punctual
and tolerant of my fretful manner
though they seem to narrow their eyes

Restlessness sets foot in me
and I set out across pastures and terraces
the moon and I breaking the hills
in a conspiracy against life un-lived

often forgetting one of us is middle-aged
(don't look at me, moon)

Perhaps I'll burn away the night
with verses to an owl's tune,
love letters to sunrise,
or how the diamonds on a wet spiderweb
glint like her eyes when she looks at the moon

It's in this way, inevitably, I get lost in things
no matter how fresh intentions might be
such is the fire that spins my shadow around
and such is the plight of an un-strict stoic
if there is such a thing

Wildflower Sigh

I'm blurry from snatches of sleep
slipping on the steepest hours
through which I'm swept

Scouting hollows of memory
carved by rivers of soft constellations
where paradise fell at our feet like dropped air
and each billowed delight
was a wildflower sigh

I've grown too old
to grapple with meaning
and I'm too busy tearing a hole
in the cage that is my sky
searching for my green
in all of that blue

Silent Danger

Humdrum duty is at my door
here to invade the space
where I try to take up none

I'm leveraging witty metaphors
in silent danger against a life that made me quiet
perhaps they're only witty to me

Winter dulls my blade but I still use it
scraping the last words out of a dream
that dream where you dance
filling up the room
radiation in the shape of sunlight
and a bowl of roses sits on the table
beside syllables carved out of love
right into the wood

Evening Falls Apart

Imposing dreams spread
as fire in my mind
collections of charged objects
but never quite defined

Folding verses into the night
feeling naked as the moon
and threadbare like the stars
with which I commune

Evening falls apart
dissonance in a trough
like clock towers across town
their timing painfully off

Door barred to unwelcome guests

as ghosts in horrid clamor

encroach my threshold to knock

with the delicacy of a thousand hammers

Backwards Devil

My regards to the moon
a little whiskey reverie at 3am
the night in all its windswept madness
is frosting my trampled edges
where the stars and I play

Wood for the fire stings my chest
as I return to my cold room
sleep is a backwards devil
dancing in the mist of my breath
but will eventually overtake me

It's here under my blanket,
slightest of movements angering my cat,
I await your return behind closed eyes
and soon you'll swoop in

graceful as a raven's glide
to knock the wind out of another dream

And when the star that lights my day
pours through the window
a soul on a string will sway in the torrent
of memories that burn my tongue at dawn

WORDS WITH WINGS

The news said today there's a hole in the sun
I shudder to think of those romantic stars being left in the cold

Maybe I'll go outside
and throw rocks at the moon
get her attention while I still can

The raging bomb of boredom has me dizzy with cabin fever
flattening out the rug only to trip over poems in a straight line

Thumbs twiddle in warm wet air and dreams are wide awake
until I go astray with words torn from my head
words with wings
singing of things I don't live

A Thousand Forgotten Nights

I must find an outside

for what is within

dissolving outlines scarcely contain

the reckoning and counting

of a paint-by-numbers existence

I must find that place

where I can rhyme my dreams

with the rocking delight of the shore

to the tune of a thousand forgotten nights

It's there I will wait

with the patience of a stone

nestled in an image

from which I can finally drink

Watercolor Dreams

I sit alone
syllables released
float like smoke in the dark
inhabiting corners where I store my soul
and loneliness dances with things I don't know

It's these times I can't sleep
I wonder how I fit
into your watercolor dreams
where you pour out bottled sunshine
and freeze rainbows right to the canvas

Do you paint us by a fire
where melancholy melts away
or is it just my footprints
amongst the roses that shout the loudest?

It's what keeps me up when night falls apart

and I long to join the winter birds

on the tail of the wind

cursing the cold

but I'd see you tomorrow

Photo by Nick Collins

Sleepwalking Poet

I cut and paste footprints
in electronic dust until I'm sick of it
growing tired of drama without theater
anguish over petty things is a slow poison
sapping the circulation of my blood

Hope is a distant lighthouse to a dissatisfied heart
that's been trampled underfoot by a web of duties
lost on the shore of a fortune-teller daydream
waiting for that beam of illumination
to swing back around

I've resigned myself to be a sleepwalking poet
this imagination is as predictable
as the tides

But right now I'm held
in the golden folds of a sunny day
holding my notebook down in the wind
and I am happy
and that is enough

Words Dug From My Pocket

Life wells forth
ambering over time
surviving my history
made me older than I am
yet still I wonder
what props up the stars

Daring to dream
adds texture to feelings
like the moss-covered memories
of drawing circles on the ground
and the way you wore the shade
of our favorite tree

I call up ghosts
when I have nothing to write
fitting them into words
dug from my pocket

This is either brave or stupid
you know I can never tel
but there's no immensity
in tame things

Dissonant Syllables

I need to find me a typewriter
one that runs on whiskey would be nice

I'll sling dissonant syllables all over
the slow quicksand of this silent feud

Invisible art in the face of indifference
my way of thinking out loud

Round and round the circle tightens
there's no roar of the crowd when you dance alone

Tonight the moon wears a devil's face
as the birds sing and I speak ill of the dead

My Words Are Smoke

Lend me an ear and I'll dress this pain
as pleasure for the release
degraded distortion of life in the cracks

A tedium self-inflicted,
chucking dreams off a cliff
the face of which holds the most scenic route

My words are smoke by the time they reclaim me,
murmurs in the abyss, and rain in my soul
echoes on the path of broken freedom

Let these lyrical gestures get swallowed by the storm
and pay no mind to heaven's threatening laugh

I dance to the rhythm of thunder

Philosophy of Lunacy

I surrender to this philosophy of lunacy
no friend of virtue to the silent upheaval
of a spoken life and its gravel smoothness

A poetic prisoner in symmetrical ignorance
to the median of days impeding the stars
from my lost gaze and half-moon halo

Outside these walls
windows ask wind for forgiveness
and winged roses are gemmed in frost
their tight cold scent
faint as a dream's sigh
and lighter than the shadows
that caress your hips

Dredger of Dreams

Starving for comfort as consternation grows sideways
I tear down old portraits and twist beauty into ache

Hot head, thin skin, a dredger of dreams
where hellhounds run and sometimes bite back

I scour my age to scrape out some use
honing velvet words against stone
and whispering wishes
that set fire to the floor

Curse of Expectation

Endlessly we drift or so it seems
just ghosts in the rain whispering our defiance
through a dissolution downpour
while impressions of life mash us down
thin as railroad pennies

So compelling this curse of expectation
muddying the ground in the courtyard of the soul

The days grow short
winter flowers open and shut in the frozen wind
and still we dance between
the golden ring of the moon and scars of time
burning our tongues on flames of love

The Latest Artificial Flavor

The smallest elements weigh the most
in the artful tension of the world's theater

Winter trees rejoice, glaring and naked
I mustn't lie here anonymous like a hair in a book

The moon she is keen, her love visible
a rope around the stars from which I swing

Scrape my eyes and peel my voice
wash the memories out with the latest artificial flavor

Running empty as roads vaster than my share unravel
drawing my own tentacled map as I chase the wind

DRUNK AGAIN

I lie down awake in a garden
amid secret fields of uncommon ground
where the Milky Way reminds me of mist in your hair

Wind cracks the mirror of the water into a thousand pieces
rage is a wasted image when the moon is just someone else's star

Solitude is a prison and these boots are heavy
but you can bet I'll be drunk again
tonight on the whitest of light

Singing to the moon of how you wore her so well
until my voice turns to dust in the dancing dawn

Photo by Liam Bolduc

Rotten Teeth

Echoes of a whippoorwill ring hollow
good morning to the midnight that still holds me

I walk a tightrope to the sun
clumsy steps in the slack action of a freight train
rumbling through my heart

Saying my peace in messages tapped out on a '74 Royal
they roll off, wandering like my mind
as they float to the floor

Think I'll make my way back down to the river
let the sound sing me to sleep as I flop on the bank
like a fish gut-hooked by a dream

Faded lines on the highway
have always been my favorite aesthetic
open to interpretation like bad tattoos
or crash test dummies

I heard an academic say
"One taste of freedom will rot your teeth out"
but little does he know I can still chew food
on the right side of my mouth just fine

WHISPERING FOX

I walk a mile out of my own way
all in the interest of saving a step

Might not be enough fuel in the tank
to unearth these poems from the levees
under which they're buried

It's 2 a.m. and the moon is bleeding
through the trees onto the ground
white coins strewn across acres of the undiscovered

I'd no intention to be long-winded
but the toothpaste is out of the tube at this point
and everyone needs to know about the blueberries
we couldn't eat because the fridge smells like fish

I add water to my zen fountain

-the cat drinks it-

and the sound reminds me of us sitting

beside the Fox River when I told you the old saying

we never step in the same river twice

Never knowing its plan we watch it gently sweep

past saplings growing at the water's edge

all the while its undermining a dam

destroying a town a few miles south of here

So much of the world laughs at magic

it makes me tired; wears me out

I need respite from pocket-sized screens of bad news

and computers that crash

So before we retire to the dreams that wait in our bed

join me beneath that milky light

to dance in the dew to the tune of the birds

that sing all night

My Own Hour

The sky seems so impassive
as I'm bogged down by the weight of the rain

I tie a leash onto a cloud
to swing over gaps in the ground
that coincidently look like graves
dark are the pine shadows
where we met at midnight

Technicolor dreams get soiled in the gray

I commune with a feeling in my own hour
where partial thoughts lie about in disarray
for this stranger to completion

Photo by Pixababy

Some Days

Some days are alright
others maybe not
some days I swing for the fences
with all I've got

Some days fly by
a blink from start to end
some caught in digital snapshots
never to be seen again

Some days it rains
oh sky please wash me clean
and some days are just mud
staining all my green

There's no use it turns out
separating good days from bad
some day they'll all be tallied up
in the twilight of the life we've had

As age catches up I find
there's not a lot I require
so pour us another round, my friend
I'll throw another log on the fire

We'll sit and trade stories
there's a million between us no doubt
glasses we'll raise to bygone days
back when we just KNEW we had it all figured out

COON HUNT

Life can be like a grandpa
well, like *my* grandpa anyway

I remember being in the swamps
on those midnight coon hunts
a pack of dogs baying bloody murder
I remember him yelling:
"Get after 'em you son of a bitch! Hya!"
He was mad for some reason

There I was ten years old thinking
maybe the dogs are trying as hard as they can
maybe they don't even want to be here
Did anyone stop to think of that?
To say I wasn't cut out for this
would be an understatement

but I wanted to be with my grandpa
show him I was as tough as him

So on through the briars and muck we'd go
black, white, and tan heads bouncing in our carbide light beams
me fighting back tears of rage each time he yelled at the dogs
or when my too-large rubber boots slid off
when they stuck in the mud
hot on the trail of some unsuspecting racoon in for a long night

I don't know where I was going when I started telling this story

I suppose the message is
don't let your world become a midnight coon hunt
and don't let life treat you like a grandpa
well, *my* grandpa anyway
driving you through a swamp of obligations
when all you want is to stop and pet the dogs
Because let's face it, just like that poor racoon,
we didn't ask for any of this shit

Now go get after it you son of a bitch!

Acknowledgements

I would like to sincerely thank you for purchasing this book. I had no idea I would ever publish a single book of my writing, let alone seven. I am fortunate to have the friends I have made in the poetry community. These folks lift me up when I am down and I am eternally grateful. Thank you all!

Most importantly I thank my love, Rae, to whom all of my books are dedicated. It's impossible to quantify what you mean to me in chasing this dream of mine. All I know is that I wouldn't trade your love, support, and encouragement for all the riches in the world.   I love you!

Sincerely,

JR (Rich) Hataway

About the Author

JR Hataway spends much of his time as a towboat captain guiding barges along the rivers and inland waterways of the United States. He found a love for poetry after being introduced to the works of Jim Harrison, Charles Bukowski, and Jack Kerouac among many others. When not on the water he can be found hiking in the woods or on a drive along the backroads of Alabama with his dog, Petey.